God spoke the world into existence in only 6 days with a few words. Jesus saved the world uttering only a few things. Can we change the world with six words or less? Dave DeVries gives it a try. Learning to speak in a concise and yet meaningful manner is a developing art form. In the day of twitter and facebook we are all learning how to say something important in 140 characters or less. The wisdom shared in this book took a whole lot longer to learn than it takes to read, so take advantage of this book!

Neil Cole, author of Organic Church and Church 3.0, and Founder and Director of Church Multiplication Associates

My friend Dave DeVries has collected his best learnings after two decades of church planting ministry and boiled them down to a collection of insightful six word statements and quotes. I am using them for inspiration, motivation, and training, as well as starters for a great discussion. You can too!

Steve Ogne, co-author of The Church Planter's Toolkit and Transformissional Coaching

Six-Word Lessons by Dave DeVries is a little book with a big message. Each six-word lesson is packed with wisdom for ministry leaders. This book is filled with succinct, easy-to-read, lessons learned from years of ministry experience. The ideas are simple but profound-- principles and practices that every healthy leader should implement. Reflecting on a chapter a day will yield insights that can bring about transformation for your life and ministry.

Bob Logan, Founder of CoachNet

I love any book or tool that makes complex issues simple and inspiring. Dave is a practitioner's sage and has dropped some well needed nuggets that any pastor or missional leader needs.

Hugh Halter, co-author of AND, Tangible Kingdom and TK Primer

Dave DeVries nails it with these pithy six word lessons. They are truths distilled from a life time of ministry and study and easily transferable to any context. Great reminders for keeping the main thing, the main thing in church planting.

Doug McClintic, Pastor of Mission and Multiplication, Fair Haven Ministries

Dave's translation of kingdom principles into missional application is necessary for any disciple or disciplemaker who wants a ministry rooted in theological thinking that matches harvest-oriented practice. In keeping his ideas and format simple, he gives us no excuse but to get to work being "doers of the Word, not merely hearers only."

Paul Kaak, Co-founder of The Organic Church Planters' Greenhouse and Associate Professor of Leadership, Azusa Pacific University

Church planters need a checklist, a series of quick reminders to keep them on a God directed course. Planting is filled with distractions provoked by the tyranny of the urgent need to "get there". Planters go 100 MPH. At such a pace it doesn't take long to miss the destination. Dave DeVries has erected a series of road signs. This is not a book to merely read...it is a book to keep close by and read again!

Bill Malick, National Director for Church Multiplication for the Christian & Missionary Alliance and Founder of The Church Multiplication Training Center

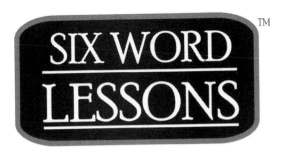

TO DISCOVER
MISSIONAL LIVING

100 Lessons
to
**Align Every Believer
with the Mission of Jesus**

Dr. David DeVries

missionalchallenge.com

Foreword by Dr. Paul Kaak

Six-Word Lessons to Discover Missional Living

Published by Leading on the Edge International
704 228th Avenue NE #703
Sammamish WA 98074
leadingonedge.com

ISBN-10: 1-933750-26-X
ISBN-13: 978-1-933750-26-2

Acknowledgements

This book is dedicated to my dad, Rev. Ray DeVries, who impacted my life in just 17 years in powerful ways. I was blessed by his love and passion for God, for the Church, and for those without Christ and without hope in this world. He taught me how to live with missional intentionality.

Thanks to those who helped me in this project. I'm grateful for the encouragement of Roland Niednagel, Keith Webb and Steve Ogne as I got started. I'm thankful for the partnership with Lonnie Pacelli, and the insights from Paul Kaak, Greg Getz, and Brian Aaby, as well as the improvement of my graphics by Elijah Hankins. I couldn't have reached completion without the support of my wife, Deanne. I thank you all – and give all praise to God for calling me to join His mission.

Contents

This Foreword Is More Than Six Words

Dave DeVries' book is full – overflowing – with gospel wisdom. Its lessons – and the contemplative space surrounding around each one – are inspired skills for living and leading with missional intention. The ideas here are not techniques, at least not in their final manifestation. In fact, they won't work if they aren't organic, authentic, life-embedded. In other words, these lessons are for people who choose to do them – will do them – even if they don't "work." They are spiritual convictions, not ways to automatically grow a ministry destined for the speaking circuit.

I had the opportunity to work closely with Neil Cole in the early developments of what many have come to know as the organic church. As Neil and I were sorting out the agrarian metaphor that – along with the Scriptures – was informing our thought, we learned a lot about good farming and good farmers. One such person is Michael Ableman who for many years was the director of Fairview Gardens in Goleta, CA. He wrote about his experiences in the book *On Good Land: The Autobiography of an Urban Farm* (1998). Of his entrée into farming, Ableman explains:

> I came to farming without training, academic credentials, books, or expectations. My grandparents had farmed but not my parents. I thought technique was important. I thought I should become masterful. Over time I discovered it was more important to learn

how to see.... By trial and error I learned and relearned until the technique I aspired to was internalized and forgotten, as technique should be... (p. 32)

As you read Dave's lessons (and as you submit to the white spaces, wandering them prayerfully), as you come to understand and practice them ("trial and error / learn and relearn") your intention is not to become masterful. Rather, we must be present to moments – with God and people – not just bursting with "vision." You must internalize them as missional disciplines and then forget them... The goal is to become like the apostle Jesus (Hebrews 3:1), lovingly obedient to the One who sends us.

In 1998 I left professional ministry after 14 years. The adjustment was a significant one for me, although not for my wife. Institutional Christian life – aligned with its own expectations and myths – was oppressive to her faith, deeper and more authentic, than mine. I had become masterful at Christian activities and especially Christian leadership. All along, she knew...she saw...something I couldn't and didn't see till after my transition. Once I began detoxing from a faith that had been rooted in performance, effectiveness, and success (I don't know if I'm ever going to be fully cleansed) my ministry really got real. There was joy in living a missional life, whether I could count the results or not! I could engage my family, my neighbors, my land, and my community to see "his kingdom come, his will be done, *on earth*, as it is in heaven."

What Dave sets out to teach us here is essential for leaders. Not so they can *produce* fruit. That's God's job. The job of leaders, and all disciples, is to *bear* fruit, to be a gallery for *Jesus the Vine* displaying the fruits if *His* life-surging energy. In fact, there will be <u>some</u> who put these ideas to work establishing churches and launching movements and <u>others</u> (just across town, perhaps) who come to the end and can't point to anything quite so tangible.

But herein is the mystery of the gospel and the gospel life. For one disciplemaker, gospel seeds will produce seedlings, which disrupt the soil, mature, and produce a harvest of organized faith communities. (A harvest, by the way, is a field full of thriving, fruitful plants. A farmer wouldn't call just one plant a "harvest." Neither should church planters!)

For another disciplemaker, more like salt and light, the result is seen in the discipleship of nations wherein the way of King Jesus permeates the culture, is diffused into the fabric of social life, and produces a fundamental transformation of values, heart, behavior, and social well-being.

We have to remember this: Jesus didn't say to plant churches. Neither did Paul, nor any of the other disciples. What Jesus said, and what his followers did, was disciple peoples. They went into the *ethne* (nations) and discipled them. How did they do this? *They made disciples of peoples by making disciples of persons*. Of course their work was not without flaw. (Although we know that "he who began a good work will complete it until the day of Christ Jesus.") We also know they didn't finish. (Yet the work goes on "to the end of the age.") What Dave hopes to teach us – what he hopes we will internalize – is that discipling nations starts with disciples who make disciples, that those disciples understand their identity as disciplemakers, and that leaders see their main work as making disciples, disciplemakers, and more disciplemaking leaders.

Dave's suggestions won't be understood as "techniques," or formulas for a ministry whose goal is financial self-sustainability. Rather, they will be gospel-wisdom, seeds planted in your heart as a disciplemaker, and which God – who causes the growth (1 Corinthians 3:6) – will germinate at the proper time.

Perhaps, as I finish my not-so-short lesson, you are now realizing something that my friend Thom Wolf understood when he served as pastor of The Church on Brady in East Los Angeles. Missionary training – which, at its heart, is what Dave offers us – is not just for those who fly away to work in another language group. Missionary training (and its ensuing results of missionary-living and missionary-leading) is for all believers. Jesus knew this (Mark 3:13-18), the people at churches like Church on Brady discovered this, and now you will too.

Finally, I haven't mentioned that Dave DeVries and I have been friends, co-seekers/students of God and his truth, and colleagues in ministry for more than 30 years. The history of our relationship is another reason why I think Dave's book is worthy of your attention and application.

Paul Kaak, St. Patrick's Day, 2010
Co-Founder, The Organic Church Planters' Greenhouse
Associate Professor of Leadership, Azusa Pacific University

Introduction

What Does "Missional Living" Look Like to Me?

In its essence *Missional Living* is simply about "embodying the mission and message of Jesus." As followers of Jesus, we seek to "be Jesus to everyone everywhere."

I wrote this book to help you embody Jesus' mission – and to help you to help others to embody Jesus' mission. Here's my "cool graphic" of what Missional Living looks like...

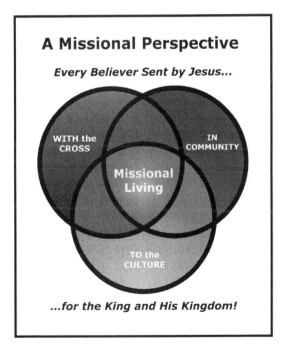

Missional Living is about being Jesus to everyone everywhere!

Every Christian has been sent on mission by Jesus to *be Jesus*!

In Acts 1:8, Jesus tells His closest followers, "But you shall receive power when the Holy Spirit has come upon you; and you shall be My witnesses both in Jerusalem, and in all Judea and Samaria, and even to the remotest part of the earth." The mission of Jesus did not begin at the ends of the earth or the other side of the planet. It started in Jerusalem, which is right where they were.

For believers today, the mission of Jesus starts right where you are. The Church does not exist to bring people in; rather it exists as those who are sent out with the mission and message of Jesus, those who are sent to be His witnesses.

> Mission is not merely an activity of the church. It is the very heartbeat and work of God. It is in the very being of God that the basis for the missionary enterprise is found. God is a sending God, with a desire to see humankind and creation reconciled, redeemed, and healed. The missional church, then, is a sent church. It is a going church, a movement of God through His people, sent to bring healing to a broken world. (Frost and Hirsch, *The Shaping of Things to Come*, p 18)

Jesus calls His followers to join Him in His mission to save the world! Jesus said, "Follow Me and I will make you fishers of men." He did not say, "Believe in me so that you can go to heaven." In fact, Jesus laid down extraordinary criteria. He

14

said, "If anyone wishes to come after Me, let him deny himself, and take up his cross, and follow Me" (Mark 8:34). He is emphatic on this condition. Unless we deny ourselves, we cannot be His disciples. "For whoever wishes to save his life shall lost it; but whoever loses his life for My sake and the gospel's shall save it" (Mark 8:35).

Jesus calls every Christian to a life of radical transformation and devotion to Christ and His mission. The sad thing is that what many Christians think is the highest level of Christianity is for Jesus the entry point.

The disciples of Jesus were not extraordinary individuals. In fact, they were described as ignorant and unlearned men. Yet it was with men like these that God began His revolution of faith, hope, and love.

The Great Commission is given to every Christ-follower, not just the pastors and elders and super-spiritual Christians!

> No one can say: 'Since I'm not called to be a missionary, I do not have to evangelize my friends and neighbors.' There is no difference, in spiritual terms, between a missionary witnessing in his hometown and a missionary witnessing in Katmandu, Nepal. We are all called to go—even if it is only to the next room, or the next block." (Thomas Hale, *On Becoming a Missionary*, p 6)

Missional Living is for every believer! To me, Missional Living is about doing my part to complete His mission while I am on this earth. It's about leading others to follow Jesus. It's about proclaiming the good news of salvation. It's about giving people the gift of eternal life. It's about seeking the lost. It's about obedience to Jesus. It's about being a good follower and helping others to follow Jesus fully.

Six-Word Lessons to Discover Missional Living is designed to help you grasp your part in God's mission. I pray that as you read this book, you will be challenged to take small, practical steps to engage in the mission – to "be Jesus" to everyone everywhere.

If you'd like to discover more ways to align with the mission of Jesus, I encourage you to *Take the Missional Challenge*. This 31-day experience will give you tangible ideas and practices to embody the gospel to everyone everywhere. Sign up at missionalchallenge.com.

I planted a church in 1990 in Southern California and now I train and coach church planters. As I've worked with new churches, I'm more and more convinced that we don't start churches to make disciples. *We start churches by making disciples.* That's our mission: making disciples.

If you're called to start a church or be part of a church planting team, this book will encourage you to keep the main thing the main thing: the mission and message of Jesus!

Christians are those who have been sent by God with the gospel to their culture. Every one of us is sent on mission with the Holy Spirit's power! And we are sent in community with other believers! When you commit to follow Jesus, you are saying, "Count me in! I am here on this earth to partner together with other Christians who are radically devoted to pursuing Christ's mission of saving the world!"

What could be better than that?

"We don't start churches to make disciples.
We start churches by making disciples."

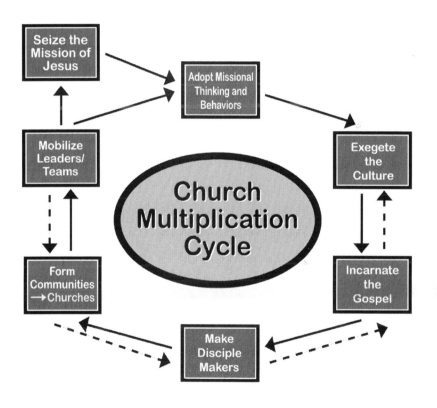

Love God.
Love People.
Make Disciples.

1

Follow Jesus. Help others follow Jesus.

Jesus said, "Follow Me and I will make you fishers of men" (Matthew 4:19).

First, follow Jesus fully. Then, help others to follow Jesus.

If you aren't helping anyone to follow Jesus – are you really following Jesus?

2

Love others like Jesus loves you.

Jesus said, "Love one another just as I have loved you" (John 13:34).

John writes, "Beloved, if God so loved us, we also ought to love one another" (I John 4:11).

So how will you love the lost, the last, and the least?

3

People are searching to know Jesus.

Look around you. People need a relationship with Jesus.

They are pursuing things that won't satisfy, trying to find what only Jesus can give them.

If you love people, then help them find Jesus. He alone satisfies.

4

Love people until they ask why.

Jesus said, "By this all people will know that you are my disciples" (John 13:35). Your love proves whose you are.

Love people so well they want to know why you love them.[i]

Is your love so tangible that it demands an explanation?

5

Discipleship starts with non-disciples, not Christians.

Too often people think "discipleship" is for new Christians.

When Jesus said, "Go and make disciples," He didn't mean to find those who are already followers and help them follow better. He sends us out to make disciples of non-disciples.

6

Christians are educated beyond their obedience.

It's not enough to know what the Bible says, we must do what it says (James 1:22). Constantly emphasize obeying what you know and the practical application of God's truth in your life[ii].

Don't just teach truth, obey it.

7

Teach people to obey Christ's commands.

The Great Commission doesn't say to "teach everything Jesus commanded." Jesus said to teach others "to obey everything I have commanded." Where do you start? 7 basic commands[iii]:

1. Repent / Believe
2. Be Baptized / Baptize
3. Love
4. Celebrate Communion
5. Pray
6. Give
7. Make Disciples

8

Key to multiplying disciples: obedient Christians.

Jesus told His disciples to make disciples who make disciples who make disciples who... (Matt 28:19-20). You're a disciple of Jesus today because of Christians who obeyed Jesus. There'll be more Christians and more churches when more Christians obey Jesus.

9

Making disciples is not an option.

Obeying the Great Commission is not optional. Jesus expected His disciples to "make disciples." And that's what they did.

So how is it that so many Christians treat Christ's commands as optional? Why is disobedience tolerated in so many churches?

10

To feed yourself spiritually: SOAP daily.

Be a Self-Feeder!

An excellent way to feed on God's Word is by reading a chapter and then writing in your journal[iv]:

- ◆ Scripture – the key verse

- ◆ Observation – what it means

- ◆ Application – what you'll do

- ◆ Prayer- talk to God

Disciples Make Disciples Who Make Disciples

11

Jesus' method was to multiply disciplemakers.

Jesus was a disciplemaker. He launched a movement of disciplemakers.

Are you part of the movement? Are you a disciplemaker?

How are you multiplying disciplemakers?

12

Disciple everyone. Equip everyone. Send everyone.

The gospel is for everyone.

Everyone needs God's grace and forgiveness. Bringing the gospel to everyone requires that everyone be discipled, equipped and sent. That's what Jesus sends everyone to do.

There are no spectators. Everyone gets in the game!

13

Discipleship begins before conversion, not after.

If disciplemaking doesn't start with the lost, you are starting in the wrong place. Starting with Christians is like fishing in an aquarium.

Disciplemaking starts by incarnating the gospel message so lost people see your hope (1 Peter 3:15).

14

Every Christian must practice disciplemaking skills.

In order to multiply disciplemakers, you must first be a disciplemaker. Every believer must embody personal disciplemaking skills. Are you?

Three Necessary Skills:

1. Follow Jesus.
2. Help others to follow Jesus.
3. Help others to help others to follow Jesus.

15

Reproduce disciples to the 4th generation.

Neil Cole notes, "Don't call it multiplication until it reaches the fourth generation."[v]

Anything prior to that is addition. Unless those whom you are discipling are actually discipling others who are making disciples, you are not multiplying.

16

The outcome of disciplemaking is disciplemakers.

Focus on making disciples and the result will naturally be disciplemakers.

If you focus on great worship, teaching, and small groups, you'll get great worship, teaching, and small groups. Yet you'll only produce disciplemakers if you focus on making disciples.

17

Make disciples any way we can.

Develop multiple approaches to making disciples.

Don't limit your thinking to ways you've seen before. Consider every way you can multiply disciplemakers. Adapt methods to your community, and discover as many ways as possible to do it.

18

Keep disciplemaking simple, practical, and reproducible.

Don't make disciplemaking complicated. Develop methods simple enough that the newest believer is employing them.

Are you helping every new believer to simply share their story and the gospel with others?

Evaluate everything you do against your desired outcome – disciplemakers.

19

Leaders must be accountable for disciplemaking.

You've heard the adage, "Speed of the leader, speed of the team."

Ask your spiritual leaders who they are influencing to follow Jesus. Don't assume they're building relationships with lost people.

When pastors and leaders are not personally making disciples, Christ's church is in danger.

20

Don't start services, start making disciples.

Church planting methods in the United States have emphasized starting services as the primary focus of starting new churches. Jesus commissions believers to make disciples, not to start services.

Planning and preparing for your first worship service won't make disciples.

Start with making disciples!

It's His Mission, What's My Part?

21

Our God is a Missionary God.

The mission of the church starts with God. God is on mission. The church joins His mission of reconciling the world to Himself.

God sent His Son on a redemptive mission, and He sends the church on a redemptive mission.

22

God's mission flows through every believer.

Jesus sends all believers as missionaries with the gospel together in community with other Christians to visibly and incarnationally display and proclaim Jesus to those in the culture around them.

Every Christian is a missionary living to fulfill His mission.

23

Pursue God's mission, not our own.

A church doesn't have its own mission – it fulfills God's mission. Every church must define and organize around God's mission in the world.

The mission of every Christian and every church is simply His mission.

24

Missional re-alignment must happen every day.

When we focus on our personal wants and desires, we abandon Jesus' redemptive mission. Following Jesus requires intentional effort to align ourselves again with Christ, and the habits and practices that actually make disciplemakers.

Daily evaluate your alignment with Jesus' mission.

25

God is working all around us.

Jesus understood this. In fact, He only did what He saw the Father doing (John 5:19).[vi]

Look for signs of hope, signs of grace, and signs of God working around you. Celebrate what God is already doing in the Harvest.

26

Jesus will teach us about mission.

While we learn about the church in Acts and the Epistles, we learn about mission in the Gospels.

Study the Gospels. That's where you will see Jesus as He accomplished His mission (John 17:4). Study Jesus. Imitate Jesus. Embody Jesus' mission.

27

Mission starts in my zip code.

You don't have to go across the sea to join in God's mission; just go across the street.

Before going anywhere, be a missionary right where you live. Start meeting needs of those around you with the love of Jesus.

28

Effective prayer focuses on Jesus' mission.

Jesus taught us to pray: "Your kingdom come, Your will be done on earth as it is in heaven" (Matthew 6:10) and "to send out workers into his harvest field" (Matthew 9:38).

Pray daily for harvest workers and His kingdom.

29

Identify God's success indicators in advance.

What is Christ's goal? Is it starting more church services or making more disciplemakers? Your answer impacts everything you do.

If you're starting services, you'll focus on getting people to come. If you're making disciplemakers, you'll focus on reproducing reproducers.

30

Every believer is sent on mission.

Every believer is sent somewhere – either to their local culture or a distant culture.

God sent Jesus to live among us; He sends us to live among the lost. This requires relationships with non-Christians. Build friendships with unbelievers in your cultural context.

Think and Act Like a Missionary

31

Hang out with and enjoy unbelievers.

That's what Jesus did. He was even called a "friend of sinners." Who are the non-Christians who would call you friend?

Instead of spending all your free time with Christians, pursue friendships with those who don't follow Christ.

32

Discover ways to bless your community.

What are the social and civic needs around you? (consider: physical, economic, social, emotional, relational, spiritual)

What one issue could you impact in the next year?

What would it look like if the kingdom of God was evident around you?

33

Missional activities start where you are.

Where's your Jerusalem (Acts 1:8)? It's where you live – with your family, your friends, and your co-workers. Start with the people closest to you. You don't have to go somewhere else first.

Be on mission right where you are.

34

Missional Transformation will require radical adjustments.

Missional Transformation is a change process that begins when believers recognize their responsibility to align themselves (passions, desires, behaviors, habits) with the missionary purpose of Jesus.

It requires radical adjustments, realigned activities, relevant approaches, and redemptive action.

35

Empty yourself of power; come empty-handed.

"We are weak in Him, yet by God's power we will live with Him to serve you" (2 Cor 13:4).

Discover ways to serve those around you. Meet genuine needs.

"Good deeds form a great bridge over which good news can travel."[vii]

36

Speak in a language people understand.

Stop talking. Listen.

Learn to speak the language of those in the culture around you. Translate the gospel into words and actions that they'll understand.

"Let us not love with words or tongue but with actions and in truth" (1 John 3:18).

37

Missional Values are evident in behaviors.

Values aren't just preferences, they are convictions. True values are demonstrated by the way you act – and seen in your checkbook and your calendar.

Missional values must be lived out consistently and influence the direction of all your activities.

38

Learn to think like an unbeliever.

You can reach people you can relate to.[viii]
The challenge many Christians face is that
the longer they've believed in Jesus, the
harder it is to relate to an unbeliever.

To reach them, learn to think like they do.

39

Jesus trained workers in the harvest.

Training happens best in the harvest.

You learn to swim in water.

You learn to drive in a car.

You learn to reach the harvest in the harvest. You learn to live missionally in your neighborhood, not in a classroom.

40

Adopt reproducible practices others can imitate.

To live missionally, discover ways to live on mission that others can do with you or like you. Habits and practices embodied together in community with other Christians will be replicated. Others will do what you do.

Discover God's Heart for Your Neighborhood

41

Loving your neighbors requires knowing them.

You can't love the people around you if you don't know who they are, and the context where they live. By researching and knowing your community in depth, you will begin to understand it, respect it, and love it.

42

Most sinners loved being around Jesus.

You need the love of Jesus everyday. Some Christians think that staying away from non-Christians will keep them from sinning.

Instead of distancing yourself from "sinners" and judging them, love them like Jesus did.

There is no impact without contact.

43

Right questions get the right answers.

Focusing on your community, ask two questions:

Who are the people? (demographic research)

What are they like? (ethnographic research)

Avoid surveys or standardized question-naires. Ask questions that naturally flow from social contexts to personal life to spiritual life.

44

Personally interview leaders in your community.

You can discover a wealth of information from others. Ask questions about...

- Hopes, aspirations, and dreams.

- Fears and problems.

- Ways you could meet needs.

- How values are formed, nurtured, and destroyed.

45

Love/Live for your city's good!

"Seek the peace and prosperity of the city to which I have carried you into exile. Pray to the LORD for it, because if it prospers, you too will prosper" (Jeremiah 29:7)

Love your city. Live for it's good!

46

Take a "tour" of your neighborhood.

What's distinct about your neighborhood and those who live there?

Walk around. Observe. Ask questions. Listen to stories. Learn idioms.

Don't hurry. Listen...and learn.

Know your community and discover what it would look like if changed by the gospel.

47

Listening to people's stories opens doors.

Listen. Ask Questions. Discover how God has already been working in drawing others to Himself.

After hearing someone's story you are better able to communicate His story in ways that help them to understand the grace of God.

48

Initiate friendships with unbelievers near you.

Many Christians don't have any non-Christian friends.

How can you build friendships?

Hospitality – invite people over

Help – meet genuine needs

Hobbies – do fun stuff together

Hangouts – go where they often go

Habits – connect through routine contact

49

Every man, woman, child needs Jesus.

Define your "Circle of Accountability"[ix] –

> [the specific geographic area for which you'll take responsibility to bring the gospel to every man, woman and child]

This focuses your activities outward, and demands that you partner with other churches to accomplish the task.

50

Identify the Harvest Force/ Harvest Field.

God accomplishes His mission through His people. Where is He working?

Assess the "Harvest Force" around you to partner for the sake of the gospel.

Look for signs of hope in your "Harvest Field" and ways to communicate the gospel.

Embody the Gospel Where You Live

51

Preach the gospel to yourself first.

Nobody needs the gospel more than you![x] Faith and repentance aren't confined to the beginning of our life in Christ; we need the gospel—we need to repent of our sins and we need to trust in Christ...daily.

52

Don't just memorize, internalize the gospel.

It's vital to know the basic message of salvation to effectively proclaim the gospel. However, just memorizing verses or an outline isn't enough; you need to practically live out the gospel in your daily life.

Be the gospel in action.

53

Imitate Jesus. Do what Jesus did.

Jesus is our Lord and Savior; yet He's also our example of how to live as a missionary.

Engage those in your life like Jesus. Serve, love, sacrifice, preach, endure, care, pray, suffer, bless, give, and make disciples like Jesus.

54

Start gospel habits, practices, and behaviors.

Living missionally isn't simply about right beliefs; it's about loving those who need Jesus.

Embody habits that demonstrate God's love in your actions to those unemployed, homeless, bereaved, sick, and abandoned; and to addicts, alcoholics, minorities, prisoners, and single parents.

55

The gospel spreads through your *oikos*.

An *oikos* is a biblical word describing the fundamental unit of society including families, friends, neighbors and associates.[xi]

The gospel spreads most effectively through close relationships. Therefore, it is vital to explore and expand relationships long before starting church services.

56

Gospel living is show and tell.

Good news and good deeds go together. If you love Jesus and enjoy fellowship with other Christians, but don't get close enough to lost people to show and then tell them the gospel – it's not good news.[xii]

57

Remember the simplicity of the gospel.

"How can they believe in the one of whom they have not heard?" (Romans 10:14). The message of the gospel is Jesus. We proclaim that Jesus is Lord. Jesus is the only way.

Jesus is the gospel; the gospel is Jesus!

58

Recognize the power of the gospel.

The gospel "is the power of God for the salvation of everyone who believes" (Romans 1:16).

It has the power to transform lives.

Lives aren't changed except by the power of the gospel.

Engaging the culture without the gospel is powerless!

59

Don't do witnessing – be a witness.

Witnessing isn't something you do – it's who you are. The Holy Spirit in your life is compelling.

Look for opportunities to tell others how your life has changed.

Your story is a powerful explanation of the gospel. Share it!

60

Everyone fails to follow Christ perfectly.

It's easy to judge others. You can always find people who fail to follow Jesus fully.

Don't forget you need God's grace and forgiveness every day. Be quick to extend grace to others today – because you'll need it too.

Church Isn't a Destination, It's People

61

The Church is God's missionary people.

"Just as God is a missionary God, so the church is to be a missionary church."[xiii]

The Church is the people of God (not the place of God) – sent with the cross in community to engage those in the culture.

62

Stop going.
Start being the Church.

Going to church doesn't make you a Christian, or define your life in Christ.

What would happen if you stopped going? How would anyone know you were a Christian?

Instead of going to church, try being the church this week!

63

Worship God.
Work for His kingdom.

"The church exists for two closely related purposes: to worship God and to work for His kingdom in the world."[xiv]

The church often gathers for corporate worship and scatters to do His kingdom work. Both matter!

Focus on both today!

64

Doing "church" isn't why church exists.

Christians are good at "doing church" on Sundays. Yet that's not what Jesus intended when He gave His life for the church.

How will you resist the pressure to simply "do" church? How will you fulfill the church's mission?

65

Life change happens best in community.

Life change happens when people can be known authentically and share their spiritual journey with others. Connecting in small groups is not optional; it's essential. Loving one another with God's love radically transforms and demonstrates His power.

66

Sent by Jesus to "Be Jesus."

You must embody Jesus' mission and message.

Essentially, every Christian is sent by Jesus to "be Jesus" to everyone everywhere.

The Missional Church is a sent church. It's not about the church sending workers; it's about the church being sent.

67

Mission exists because worship does not.

"Missions is not the ultimate goal of the church. Worship is. Missions exists because worship doesn't. Worship is ultimate, not missions, because God is ultimate, not man."[xv]

The redeemed will worship God eternally. Yet now we must pursue God's mission.

68

The church is leaving the building.

The Church in the United States is declining, dysfunctional, fragmented, marginalized, and internally focused. This is a direct consequence of neglecting its mission.

To accelerate Christ's mission, the church needs to get out of the building and into the world.

69

Starting churches requires removing the "Queen."

Rookie chess players overuse their Queen. Surrendering it at the start of a game will teach you to value the other pieces.

In a similar way, many churches depend exclusively on Sunday services (Queen) to accomplish everything. Discover the other pieces.

How will you use them?

70

Your church isn't God's only church.

Where is the Body of Christ on mission in your community?

Thank God for their ministry.

Learn from them about specific needs.

Discover how the gospel is being incarnated.

Identify potential ways to partner together.

Pray for them.

Time To Take the Missional Challenge!

71

Seize Christ's mission as your own.

Every believer's mission is the same. There is one mission.

You don't need to discover Christ's mission for your church or for your life. You simply need to embrace Christ's redemptive mission as your own. Carpe missio!

72

Incarnate the gospel wherever you are.

Don't start a program. Adopt incarnational practices instead.

Care for the physical needs of those around you. Like the Good Samaritan, get up off your "donkey" and start meeting needs. Be the hands and feet of the gospel.

73

Be Jesus to everyone around you.

Embody Jesus!

Incarnate, exemplify, represent, personify, demonstrate, typify, show, explain, prove, confirm, illustrate, epitomize, display, exhibit, verify, attest, substantiate, authenticate, express, characterize, and be...the gospel to those where you live, where you work and where you play.

74

Exegete the culture to communicate effectively.

If you are going to impact those in your culture, you must first study the culture. Once you have exegeted the culture, you are able then to contextualize the gospel message so that it is understood as good news.

75

Plant the gospel in the culture.

The gospel is good news! Live out the good news that trusting in Jesus alone restores relationship with God.

Don't start planting a church. Start planting the gospel. As the gospel takes root and changes lives, plant a church.

76

Demonstrate and declare hope in Jesus.

Hell is real and people are going there. Hell is their eternal destiny without Jesus.

You have the answer. Jesus is their only hope. Without Him, it's hopeless.

This should compel you to show and tell others about Jesus!

77

Multiply disciples who keep multiplying disciples.

The foundational and most critical of all missional behaviors is disciplemaking. Why?

Because Christ sent the church to make disciples. And without disciplemaking, the church ceases to exist. This is Christ's redemptive strategy. Missional activity starts with and continues through disciplemaking!

78

Motivate/Mobilize everyone to join you.

Every believer must make disciples.

Everyone without Jesus must have an opportunity to accept or reject the gospel.

You never know who God will use, so keep training everybody.

Missional movements in America will require that every believer join in.

79

Orient your life around Christ's agenda.

You have your own agenda. You focus on things that matter to you.

What is it that you need to drop in order to better align with the mission of Jesus?

How will you impact your neighbors with the gospel?

80

Pursue Missional Alignment: Cross + Community + Culture

Jesus sends every believer...
    with the Cross...
        in Community...
            to the Culture...
                for the King and His Kingdom.

Every Christian, aligned with Jesus' missionary heart, is to incarnationally display the gospel to those around them and make disciples.

Lessons I Learned Planting a Church

81

God's in control
and I'm not.

The problem is that I want to be in control and I'm not. However, because God is sovereignly in control, I can trust Him completely in every situation.

Psalm 115:3: "Our God is in heaven; He does whatever pleases Him."

82

God is not in a hurry.

When embodying missional living, it is so easy to get impatient and frustrated when there are not instant results or immediate progress. God has perfect timing and isn't hurried. We need to learn to wait and to keep trusting.

83

Your character development precedes ministry accomplishment.

Being precedes doing.[xvi] Who I am is more important than what I do for God.

Pay attention to your team's character formation, not just the tasks to plant a church. Failing to focus on inner life development will hinder effectiveness.

84

Never assume people are okay spiritually.

Belonging together in community demands mutual accountability. Jesus says that a tree is known by its fruit. Look for fruit.

Share what's going on inside and ask the questions that no one else is asking instead of assuming everything is okay.

85

God's plans are better than mine.

I don't have to dream up things that I want to do for God—I just need to join Him in what He's already doing. That's success!

86

Your family = your most important ministry.

It's easy to give priority to other's needs over your responsibility for your own family. Church planting requires sacrifice, but don't sacrifice your family.

Make your family your highest priority. Be there! Failure at home means failure in ministry.

87

Train in ministry, not for ministry.

Leadership development is not a program, it is a lifestyle. Learning to serve others does not happen in the classroom, but in the context of ministry.

All believers must be equipped and empowered at every opportunity right where they live.

88

You're responsible for your own growth.

If you aren't ensuring that you're maturing spiritually, no one else will. It's your job—pay attention to yourself.

Don't wait to be taught or mentored. Seek out what you need. Own your personal development. Take steps daily toward growth.

89

The goal is disciples, not decisions.

Often evangelism results in decisions for Christ, not disciples of Christ. There is a big difference!

Jesus was a disciplemaker. He didn't call people to decisions; He called them to make disciples.

How will you make disciples who make disciples?

90

Never start anything without a team.

Whether starting a church, a ministry, or outreaches—always involve a team.

Accomplishing the mission of Jesus requires teams of believers to multiply disciples and churches all over the place.

You cannot do it alone! You need a team.

Don't Skip Reading the Final Chapter

91

Nobody will drown in my neighborhood.

Every Christian's on a lifesaving mission. Do you "own" the mission?

God alone saves, but you can ensure that everyone around you has an opportunity to see how your life's been changed by Jesus. You can "own" your world.

92

The kingdom of God is "glocal."

The Church and Christianity are "glocal."xvii

Not just global – which sounds like it's over there somewhere.

Not just local – which sounds like it's only here.

Christ's mission embraces both local and global at the same time. How will you?

93

It's about cookies, not cookie jars.

Don't focus on your great cookie jar, and forget it's about cookies.

Creating a great "container" and hoping people leave their cookie jar because yours is better is ridiculous.

You don't need a cookie jar if you aren't making cookies.

94

Focusing on less is more effective.

Choose to do fewer things, but things which have greater impact.

Limiting yourself to the essential will maximize your time and energy.

To embody missional living, start by following Jesus and helping someone else to follow Jesus!

95

You cannot force growth and multiplication.

The key to missional movements is multiplication at every level. Multiply everything.

Addition is fast – multiplication is slow. It takes time.

Start making disciples who will make disciples and growth and multiplication will eventually happen all by itself (Mark 4:28).

96

You need more than the Bible.

To embody missional living, you need more than the Bible.

You need the power of the Holy Spirit.

You need the love of Jesus.

You need the grace of God.

Don't just give people the Bible – give them Jesus!

97

On the job.
Just in time.

Learning to embrace missional practices doesn't happen in the classroom, but in the context of mission. Not in the barn, but in the harvest field.

To embody missional living, start living on mission right now right where you are.

98

Every church planter needs a coach.

If you're planting a church, get a coach right away.[xviii]

A Christian coach is someone who comes alongside a planter to navigate the challenges faced in starting out.

Coaches help you to fully live out God's calling in your life!

99

Few leaders in ministry finish well.

According to Bobby Clinton, only about 30% of the leaders in Scripture finished well. [xix]

What will you do to finish well? Keep your relationship with God strong. Keep learning and growing. Keep developing godly character. Stay focused on God's mission.

100

God's "Well Done" is worth it!

What matters most when your life is over is whether you joined God in His mission.

Don't wait until your last days to align with Jesus' mission – start now. Hearing God say "Well Done"xx is worth giving your life to!

See the entire Six-Word Lesson
Series at *6wordlessons.com*

*Learn more about Missional Living
and Dr. David De Vries at
missionalchallenge.com*

Interested in coaching?

davedevries.org

Notes

[i] Joe Aldrich, *Gentle Persuasion*.

[ii] Bob Logan first introduced me to this concept.

[iii] George Patterson & Richard Scoggins, *Church Multiplication Guide*, p. 17.

[iv] Wayne Cordeiro, enewhope.org/firststeps/journaling/

[v] Neil Cole, Reproducing Churches (lecture).

[vi] Henry Blackaby, *Experiencing God*, p. 15.

[vii] Rick Rusaw & Eric Swanson, *The Externally Focused Church*, p. 61.

[viii] Rick Warren, Saddleback Conference 1990.

[ix] Dwight Smith & Robert Mountford, *Finding God's Purpose for the Church*, p. 34.

[x] Dave & Debbie Walker taught this at OC Internship 2007.

[xi] Bob Logan & Neil Cole, *Beyond Church Planting*, p. 43.

[xii] Joe Aldrich, *Gentle Persuasion*.

[xiii] Craig Van Gelder, *The Essence of the Church*, p. 98.

[xiv] N.T. Wright, *Simply Christian*, p. 211.

[xv] John Piper, *Let the Nations Be Glad*, p. 17.

[xvi] Bobby Clinton, *The Making of a Leader*, p. 13.

[xvii] Paul Kaak first introduced me to this concept.

[xviii] Sign up for a complimentary coaching session at davedevries.org.

[xix] Bobby Clinton, bobbyclinton.com.

xx Matthew 25:21

Made in the USA
Lexington, KY
21 December 2012